AFRICAN
FOOD AND DRINK

Martin Gibrill

Wayland

FOOD AND DRINK

British Food and Drink
Caribbean Food and Drink
Chinese Food and Drink
French Food and Drink
Greek Food and Drink
Indian Food and Drink
Italian Food and Drink
Japanese Food and Drink

Jewish Food and Drink
Mexican Food and Drink
Middle Eastern Food and Drink
North American Food and Drink
Russian Food and Drink
South East Asian Food and Drink
Spanish Food and Drink
West German Food and Drink

Editors: Susannah Foreman and Clare Chandler

First published in 1989 by
Wayland (Publishers) Limited
61 Western Road, Hove
East Sussex BN3 1JD, England

British Library Cataloguing in Publication Data
Gibrill, Martin
  African food and drink.
  1. Africa. Food. Drinks. Food & drinks
  I. Title
  641'.096

  ISBN 1–85210–465–1

Typeset by DP Press, Sevenoaks
Printed in Italy by G. Canale & C.S.p.A., Turin
Bound in France by A.G.M.

Cover *Citrus fruits for sale at Freetown market, Sierra Leone.*

Contents

Africa and its people

Africa is a very large continent. Its vast plains and plateaux, deserts, tropical savannah (grass and shrub land) and equatorial rainforests, make it both an exciting and a varied region. Africa covers 30 million square km and has 25,600 km of coastline; it is 3.5 times the size of the USA and larger than China and India put together. This book concentrates on food in tropical Africa because it is impossible to cover adequately the wide range of different foods and lifestyles that occur throughout the continent.

The population of sub-Saharan Africa is approximately 400 million people, 100 million of whom live in Nigeria. The density of population varies dramatically, but in general it is half as densely populated as the world's average. Africa is the least urbanized of the continents, although there has been an increasing drift of people towards its cities in the last twenty years. Many cities have doubled their populations in under a decade. The

The snow-capped peak of Mount Kilimanjaro dominates the Kenyan plains.

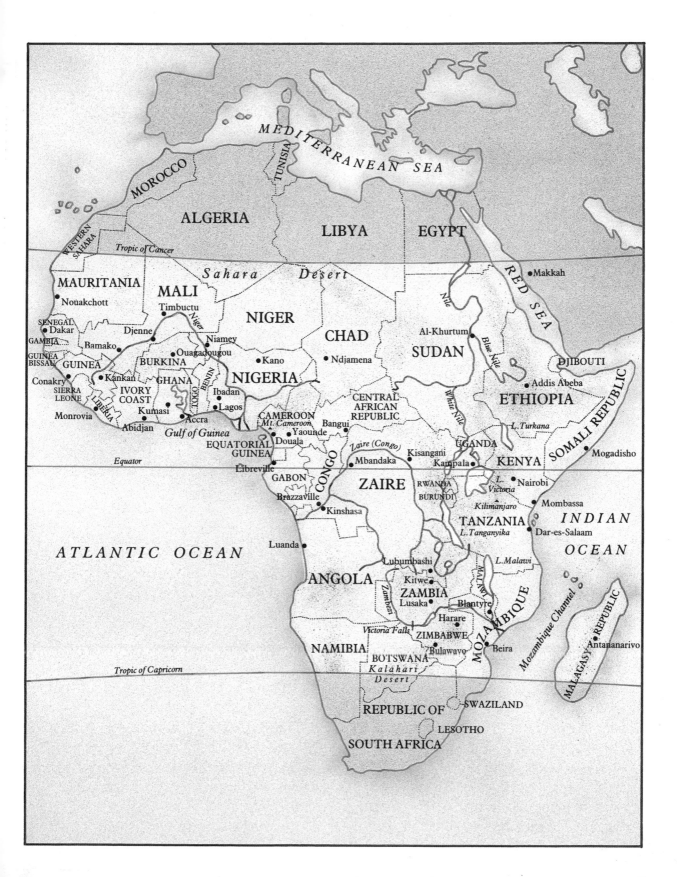

MEDITERRANEAN SEA

MOROCCO

TUNISIA

ALGERIA

LIBYA

EGYPT

WESTERN SAHARA

Tropic of Cancer

Sahara   Desert

RED SEA

Makkah

MAURITANIA

MALI

NIGER

CHAD

SUDAN

Al-Khurtum

Nouakchott

Timbuctu

Niger

DJIBOUTI

SENEGAL
Dakar

Djenne

Niamey

Ndjamena

Blue Nile

Addis Abeba

GAMBIA

Bamako

Ouagadougou

Kano

Kano

ETHIOPIA

GUINEA
BISSAU

BURKINA

GUINEA

NIGERIA

CENTRAL
AFRICAN
REPUBLIC

White Nile

SOMALI REPUBLIC

Conakry

Kankan

GHANA

BENIN

Ibadan

L. Turkana

SIERRA
LEONE

IVORY
COAST

TOGO

Lagos

CAMEROON

UGANDA

Monrovia

LIBERIA

Kumasi

Accra

Mt. Cameroon

Bangui

Kisangani

Mogadisho

Abidjan

Gulf of Guinea

Yaounde

Kampala

KENYA

EQUATORIAL
GUINEA

Douala

Zaire (Congo)

Mbandaka

Equator

Libreville

RWANDA

*L.
Victoria*

Nairobi

GABON

CONGO

ZAIRE

BURUNDI

INDIAN

Brazzaville

Kilimanjaro

Mombassa

Kinshasa

TANZANIA

OCEAN

Luanda

L. Tanganyika

Dar-es-Salaam

ATLANTIC OCEAN

Lubumbashi

L. Malawi

Mozambique Channel

ANGOLA

Kitwe

ZAMBIA

MALAWI

MALAGASY REPUBLIC

Zambezi

Lusaka

Blantyre

MOZAMBIQUE

Antananarivo

Harare

Victoria Falls

ZIMBABWE

Beira

NAMIBIA

Bulawayo

BOTSWANA
*Kalahari
Desert*

Tropic of Capricorn

REPUBLIC OF

SWAZILAND

LESOTHO

SOUTH AFRICA

5

The Tsavo national park in Kenya.

population of Kinshasa in Zaïre, for example, increased from 900,000 to 2,000,000 in just seven years.

Throughout such a vast continent the climatic conditions vary considerably: the western slopes of Mount Cameroon (4,070 m) have the second highest rainfall in the world, whereas the Sahara and Kalahari Deserts might not see rain for years at a time. The temperature can rise to as high as 45°C in north-west Africa and, at the other extreme, the sub-zero temperatures at the peak of Mount Kilimanjaro in Tanzania (5,791 m) mean that it is always snow-capped.

The terrain includes rainforest,

where trees grow up to 70 m high. There are also numerous lakes and rivers, including Victoria Falls (the highest and widest waterfall in the world) on the Zimbabwean and Zambian border and the Rivers Nile (6,700 km) and Niger (over 4,000 km). The Rift Valley, which is the result of a geographical fault, is one of the most interesting sights. It runs from Jordan in the Middle East down through Ethiopia, Kenya and Tanzania into Mozambique. It is about 8,700 km long (over a quarter of the earth's circumference). In the north it separates the Middle East from Africa. In Kenya the walls of the rift rise to 1,220 m in places.

There are hundreds of different ethnic groups in Africa. An ethnic group is a group in which members

Harare in Zimbabwe. Over the past twenty years the population of Africa has drifted increasingly from the rural areas toward the cities.

have a common identity and, sometimes, allegiance; it also, usually, has a common culture. For example, the nomadic Masai of Kenya live in a completely different way to that of their close neighbours the Kikuyu, who cultivate the land and do not roam. The savannah areas in East and West Africa have encouraged some ethnic groups to mix, whereas the dense, uncontrollably fertile forests have traditionally served as refuge zones for less powerful groups and, consequently, discouraged ethnic groups from mixing.

The ethnic pattern in Africa was complicated by the arrival of other groups from Europe and Asia. They included people of Arab descent, whose ancestors traded in, and eventually settled along, the East African coast 1,500 years ago; the Asians (who were imported as indentured labour in the last century by the British); and the Europeans who traded in, and eventually colonized, parts of Africa in the nineteenth century. The Mistos of Angola and Mozambique are a racial mix of Europeans and Africans.

The colonization by Europeans of parts of Africa in the nineteenth

Dr Richard Leakey excavates the skull of a human thought to have lived hundreds of thousands of years ago in Kenya.

and early twentieth centuries while only being a very short episode in Africa's long history, has, unfortunately, sometimes obscured Africa's cultural heritage. It is now considered possible that the first human beings lived in Africa. The search to explain how the human race developed was advanced by the discovery of the remains of a twelve-year-old boy on the shores of Lake Turkana in northern Kenya. The boy's remains, which were preserved by the swampy conditions, cannot be accurately dated, but they could be as old as 300,000 years. This discovery, along with other findings, has led scientists to believe that the genesis of 'thinking man' was in Africa.

The famous kingdoms of Mali, Benin (Nigeria), Greater Zimbabwe and Ashante (Ghana) are just a few examples which show the African cultural achievement. There is evidence that learning and education was highly valued by many Africans in the past, as it is also today. A Spanish Muslim traveller in the sixteenth century reported that there was more money to be made from selling books in Timbuctu than from any other items. Many Europeans believed that Africa lacked any cultural heritage and, consequently, the discovery of a royal *kraal* (court) in Zimbabwe, which dates back to the ninth century AD, was initially greeted with disbelief by its European 'discoverers'. They would not believe that it had African origins, and preferred to think it was the work of Phoenician explorers.

Music plays an important role in the African way of life. It varies from the more traditional, complex rhythmic beating of drums and groups singing intricate harmonies, to modern High Life, with its electric guitars and electronic keyboards. African music is not only important throughout the continent but it has also a significant influence on Western music, particularly jazz.

African art is very distinctive and highly valued: priceless pieces of African art can be seen in museums throughout the world. The Cubist movement of the early twentieth century was influenced by the art of the Niger people of West Africa. Pablo Picasso was the best-known artist of this movement.

There are as many as 2,000 African languages spoken throughout Africa and it is not uncommon for individuals to be fluent in two or three of these; many of these languages are spoken only with no written form. The official languages spoken in sub-Saharan Africa, however, are English, French, Portuguese and Arabic. Apart from their international significance and their use as official languages of communication, they also represent, with the exception of Arabic, a legacy of Africa's colonial past. Although children are taught at school through one of the official languages, they generally speak others at home. For

instance, Swahili is the preferred language of millions of people in East Africa.

There are three major religious influences in Africa: traditional religions, Islam and Christianity. African traditions are still strong and include initiation rites, fertility

A Masai mother with her child. The Masai, who live on the Kenyan plain, are a nomadic people.

The famous Djenne Mosque in Mali.

rites and belief in a supreme god, although, with the exception of the Akan people of Ghana and a few other groups, they do not worship God. Ancestors are often worshipped. Many of these religions also believe that natural objects such as trees, rocks, mountains and rivers have a spirit, just as they believe human beings do, but to a lesser degree. In some instances, these traditional religions have borrowed from Islamic practices. None of the African religions became universal, but a number of them are just as complex as Christianity or Islam.

Islam was introduced in sub-Saharan Africa by Arab traders between the twelfth and thirteenth centuries AD and many Africans, particularly those living on the edge of the Sahara Desert, are Muslim. Islam originated in the Middle East; its founder and inspiration was an Arab named Muhammad. The famous mosque at Djenne in Mali reflects Islam's influence in Africa. Today Islam has the fastest growing number of converts in Africa. The introduction of Christianity was announced by European explorers, missionaries and settlers. They came from countries such as Germany, Britain, France, Belgium and Portugal.

11

Agriculture, transport and markets

Tropical Africa has the potential to feed itself. However, a combination of droughts, floods, disease and pests such as the tsetse fly and locust (which are a threat particularly to north and west Africa) have hampered the efforts of African countries to feed their populations. Wars have made the situation much worse in some areas. The policy of producing cash crops such as cotton, which use valuable agricultural land, has also affected the African peoples' ability to feed themselves.

Throughout Africa there is a strong tradition of living off the land. Apart from farming the land and tending cattle, sheep, goats and pigs, there are still many Africans who hunt or gather vegetation for food. However, hunting for food is now less widespread.

Nomadic peoples, such as the

The nomadic Fulani of West Africa roam over large areas with their cattle.

Women in Tanzania working the land.

Masai and the Fulani, tend herds of cattle and goats, which graze throughout large areas of east or north-west Africa. Although the cattle are a source of food, they are also seen as a form of wealth and status. Often they are used as a form of money with which to barter, and are also killed for important ceremonial occasions. These cattle yield very little meat and milk compared to cattle reared on ranches. They are also prone to a wide range of diseases.

Methods of land cultivation can be divided into two major categories: large scale commercial farming and subsistence farming. Subsistence farming is when an individual, family or community produce only enough food for their own needs. In many areas women are the subsistence farmers, while the men work in the towns, mines and factories. Food grown for personal and family consumption is harvested and stored on an individual basis, although in some communities there are village or communal storage places. As much as 60 per cent of the agricultural land is used primarily for subsistence farming. In Zaïre and Nigeria, however, nearly 80 per cent of the land still remains uncultivated.

Subsistence farmers may cultivate a piece of land for a few years before moving on to another patch. It is necessary for them to move because the land becomes exhausted and loses its ability to supply the crops with the essential nutrients they need in order to grow. This process is called bush fallow farming. One example of this method of farming is known as the 'chitemene' system and is practised

Women workers sifting coffee beans before they are left to dry. They work for a Kenyan coffee co-operative.

in Zambia. In forested or heavily vegetated areas, the trees and vegetation are burnt. This clears the land and the ash from the trees provides potash, which is a good fertilizer.

Large plantations, particularly in East Africa, are farmed on a commercial basis. They grow cash crops, which are crops that are specifically grown because they can be sold to other countries, as well as in local markets. Cash crops earn money for the businesses and bring money into the country. These plantations grow a wide range of produce. For example, on plantations in Tanzania and Kenya tea, coffee and tobacco are grown; in Angola and Uganda tea, sugar and sisal are grown. Cocoa, coffee and palm products are grown throughout West Africa. As with the Kenyan plantations, West African plantations do not just produce food crops: rubber is also produced in Nigeria and Liberia.

In between the huge plantations and the small scale subsistence farmer are the co-operatively managed farms. A co-operative is a business run and managed by the workers, who also produce the goods, perform a service or work the fields. In Tanzania a series of co-operatives have linked together for coffee production and provide services which range from growing, storing and transporting the beans, to marketing them.

The Ghanaian cocoa co-operatives have enabled Ghana to produce 30 per cent of the world's cocoa. Co-operative methods of production are spreading in Africa and are one of the ways in which Africans are farming on a larger scale. A major problem for all food producers, whether they are large or small, is getting their produce to market. Because rail and road networks are not very extensive, farms are usually sited near towns, existing roads or railway stations. In some countries, however, the roads and railways have fallen into disrepair because of wars or lack of money.

Countries that are completely landlocked, such as Uganda and Zambia, must rely on their neighbours' goodwill if they want to export their goods by rail and ship (which is a much cheaper form of transportation than aeroplane). Small market traders, who do not possess motorized transport, often carry their produce to market or transport it by ox and cart or by bicycle.

Rivers are also used to transport goods. The River Niger, which winds through a number of West African states, is used for local trade. Zaïre has over 14,000 km of navigable waterways, but the problem with many rivers is that they either dry up at certain times during the year or they are full of waterfalls. Sometimes they are simply not wide or deep enough for a boat to travel along.

The need for refrigeration is important in Africa as food has to be transported long distances. It is essential for traders who do not have refrigerated lorries to get their produce to market as quickly as possible.

Markets have played an important part in African life. The large ones are located on important trade routes and can usually be found in the centre of towns. The market at Timbuctu in Mali, for example, is famous for the role it played as a trading centre. Herbs, salt and spices, which were transported on camel across the desert by Arab traders, were exchanged for gold from the twelfth century onwards.

Anything from fruit and vegetables to transistor radios and cameras are sold in the markets. The smell of herbs and spices, freshly barbecued plantain or meat, and livestock fills the air. Despite the growth of western-style cities, the market place has managed to retain much of its importance as a focal point in many African towns.

Although it is unwise to generalize for so many countries, women usually play a significant

These traders are taking their bananas to market by bicycle.

King Jimmy market in Sierra Leone, West Africa. Most of the stall holders are women.

role in the running of these markets. The Ashanti women of Ghana have control over the running of the markets in their region. In markets in other regions women often manage stalls alongside men.

The staple diet

A staple diet refers to the principal food on which a people rely for their daily nourishment. Staples form the main part of the meal and are eaten at any time of the day. In contrast to western countries, meals in Africa are less likely to be divided into breakfast, lunch, tea and dinner.

The staple diet varies through-out sub-Saharan Africa mainly according to the climate. The amount of rainfall an area receives and its frequency is very important, because certain crops need more water than others. The cultivation of rice, for example, requires a great deal of water and it is therefore grown only in three main regions: West Africa, Kenya and the Central African Republic, and Zaïre.

In areas where there is more than 1,250 mm of rain per year, rice, oil

Tomatoes and yams grow particularly well in West Africa's tropical climate.

Maharagwe (Spiced red beans)

You will need:
½ kg dried red beans
2 medium onions, chopped
2–3 tomatoes, peeled and chopped
1–2 tablespoons of oil
2 tablespoons of turmeric
1½ teaspoons of cayenne pepper
½ l coconut milk (see p. 34)

What to do:
(1) Cover the beans with plenty of water and boil vigorously for 10 minutes. Discard all the water. Put the beans back into the saucepan and add ½ l of water. Allow to boil and then simmer until nearly tender (approximately 1 hour – add more water, if necessary). Drain off the water. (2) Sauté the onions until golden. (3) Add coconut milk and mix the onions and the remaining ingredients with the beans. Bring to the boil and allow to simmer for 5–10 minutes, until the beans are tender. (4) Serve *maharagwe* in a bowl with a slice of bread or some fried sliced plantain.

Serves 4–6

A woman stirs maize meal to make the traditional Kenyan dish of ugali. *It is used to scoop up the stew.*

palms, yams, sweet potatoes, bananas and plantain form the staple food. Where the rainfall is below 1,250 mm but above 250 mm, cereals such as wheat and corn and various types of beans, are important. In the remaining areas the growing of any staple is dependent on irrigation schemes and in these, date palms and millet are often grown.

A combination of the cereal staples and any of the beans or peas (sometimes called pulses) provides an individual with a balanced diet, especially if eaten with a green vegetable. The grain staples provide starch (carbohydrates) and the pulses provide protein, which are the main requirements for a healthy diet. Staples form the main part of the meal and are eaten at any time of the day.

The most widely grown staple foods are sorghum (a type of corn), cassava and maize, because these can tolerate a wide range of climatic conditions. They can grow in tropical conditions as well as semi-arid ones. Sorghum is thought to have originated in Africa. The other grains were introduced to the continent by Arabs, Indians and Portuguese, although there is some argument about whether maize was introduced to, or originated in, Africa.

These and other staple foods are pounded into a soft sticky mass with the addition of water or, sometimes, milk. The result looks a bit like semolina. A spicy stew of meat or fish is served to accompany such dishes, because they can taste very bland. The staples are not always served as the main meal;

A woman making cassava balls from crushed cassava. The balls are usually fried and eaten with a spicy stew.

they are also used in the preparation of desserts and snacks. Cassava, maize and sorghum can be ground and used as flour. In Zimbabwe they make sweet potato cookies and in West Africa grilled plantain with red pepper is often served as a snack.

There is a strong vegetarian tradition in Africa, particularly amongst groups of people who live a nomadic existence. Although they hunt, they also collect fruit, nuts and leaves. The Pygmies of the Congo Basin are one of the groups who hunt and gather fruits. The Masai diet consists mainly of milk and meat.

Fufu

You will need:
½ kg cassava

What to do:
(1) Peel the cassava and leave to soak in water for 4 days. They will now be soft.
(2) Cut out the central hard core. Place in a pan and cover with water. Bring to the boil and then allow to simmer for 10 minutes. (3) Lift the cassava out of the saucepan and put into a mortar. Pound them with a pestle them until they form a soft dough. (4) Place the dough on a dish. *Fufu* should be served with meat or fish stew.

Safety note: Be careful when peeling the cassava and removing them from the hot water. Ask an adult to help.

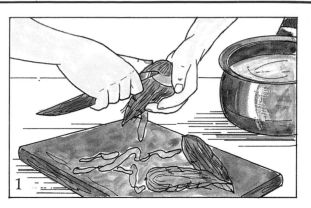

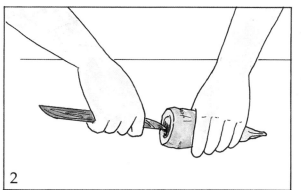

West Africa

The main staples eaten in this area are cassava, yam, sweet potatoes, couscous and rice. Yam and sweet potatoes are root vegetables, which means that they grow beneath the ground. Couscous (a form of wheat) and rice are grains or cereal. Couscous is also widely eaten throughout North Africa and was probably introduced by the Arabs to West Africa. It is usually cooked by steaming rather than boiling. Although couscous and rice are often cooked and eaten without being pounded, they are used, as well as cassava, plantain or yam, as the ingredient for *fufu*. *Fufu* is the result of one of these staples being boiled and then pounded with a large mortar and pestle into a soft, sticky mass. (It is eaten in many of the West African countries.)

In parts of West Africa rice is the main staple food. Rice is particularly popular because it is easy to store and transport. One of the famous dishes of the area is based on rice and gets its name from the Wolof people of Senegal. It is called *jollof* rice and is a mixture of rice with chicken and meat – rather like an Italian risotto or a Spanish paella. (See page 39).

Pounded yam with fish soup cooked in palm oil.

Central Africa

The main staple foods in this region are cassava, maize and sweet potato. Rice is grown in parts of Zaïre. In Zaïre *bidia* is made, which is like a stiff porridge and is made by pounding cornmeal. Sometimes tapioca flour is also added. This dish is also made in other parts of Central and East Africa and is known as *ugali* in Kenya and *nsima* in Malawi and Zambia. Apart from being mashed, these vegetables and fruits are sometimes fried, grilled, as in the case of plantain, or cut into pieces and boiled.

East Africa

In parts of Africa where there are longer periods without rain, staples such as maize, varieties of millet and sorghum prosper. Millet and sorghum are the traditional cereals and they have the advantage of being able to withstand drought better than maize. However, there are regional variations. In Tanzania and Kenya sweet potatoes are widely available. Cassava is the most important root crop because it

Bidia

You will need:
225 ml milk
250 g white cornmeal
225 ml water

What to do:
(1) Heat the water in a saucepan. While the water is being heated, mix 125 g of cornmeal with the milk in a jug until it forms a smooth paste. You will need to mix vigorously. (2) Carefully add the mixture to the boiling water and stir. Gradually add the remaining cornmeal and allow to cook for another 3–4 minutes. You should be stirring the mixture all the time. The mixture will get heavier and begin to form a mass. (3) Remove it from the saucepan and put into a bowl. You may wish to shape it into a large ball by hand before serving. Make sure your hands are slightly wet so that the mixture does not stick to them. (4) Serve with meat or fish stew.
Serves 4
Safety note: Ask an adult to help you when adding the mixture to the boiling water.

Assorted fish are boxed ready for sale near Accra in Ghana.

can tolerate semi-arid conditions for short periods. It flourishes in Malawi. In parts of Uganda where there is not a prolonged dry season, bananas are the main staple crop. A similar process to that of making *fufu* applies in the preparation of *matoke*, a Ugandan dish made from plantain.

Fishing

Apart from the thousands of kilometres of coast, there are hundreds of lakes and rivers in which Africans can fish. In Tanzania and Kenya the lakes and the rivers (including Lake Victoria, which is the second largest lake in the world) are the main source of fish for the local population. Only 10 per cent of the fish caught come from the sea, even though Tanzania and Kenya have a combined coastline of over 950 km. Fishing is usually performed from open canoes with gill nets. Fish are sun-dried, smoke-dried or salted to preserve them before being transported to market. The fishermen and their families eat a proportion of the catch. Malawi, which is landlocked, has a fish catch higher than that of its neighbour Mozambique, which has a coastline.

Unlike its East African counterparts, Angola's coastline is a rich source of fish because the sea is relatively shallow there. Fishing operates on a much more commercial basis, with catches being turned into fishmeal for export as well as being dried and transported inland. The types of fish caught include anchovies, sardines and mackerel.

Fish forms an important part of the West African diet. Two-thirds of the region's catch comes from the sea. However, Mali, which is landlocked, catches nearly 7 per cent of the region's fish from the River Niger. Most of them are caught from large open canoes, which are either paddled or sailed, with nets or long lines for those fish which swim at greater depths. As in other parts of Africa the fish is dried or salted. There are some processing plants and a small number of deep-sea fishing fleets.

Influences on African food

The camel caravans that once crossed the Sahara Desert were one of the first major influences on African food. The traders exchanged salt and other goods for gold. The Akan people of the forests of Ghana were heavily involved in this trade. A Scottish explorer, Mungo Park, who traced

Ghanaian women with strings of very large snails for sale.

Groundnut stew

You will need:

1 kg chuck beef, cut into small pieces
2–3 medium onions, chopped
8 okra, chopped
3 tablespoons of tomato purée
3 tablespoons of peanut butter
3 medium tomatoes
1 teaspoon of cayenne pepper
¾ l water

What to do:

(1) Using a saucepan, fry the meat until it is sealed (it should be brown on all sides). Put the meat into a large pan and add water. Bring to the boil and allow to simmer for about 1½ hours until the meat begins to soften (you can tell by sticking a fork into it). Remove the meat with a slotted spoon. Set aside the meat and retain the stock. (2) Add onions to the pan in which the meat was sealed and allow to brown. Stir in the tomato purée and add the tomatoes, salt and pepper. Allow to simmer for 5 minutes. (3) Meanwhile, mix the peanut butter in a jug with the stock until it is a smooth paste. You will find it easier if you mix a small amount at a time. The okra should be washed and cooked in a separate pan until they are soft (about 5 minutes). Carefully add the onion mixture, along with the meat and okra, to the pan. Bring back to the boil and allow to simmer for 20 minutes. (4) This dish can be served with rice or *fufu*.
Serves 4–5

Safety note: Be careful with sharp knives when chopping vegetables. Ask an adult to help.

Western cuisine is available in many parts of Africa, particularly in the tourist areas.

the path of the River Niger in the middle of the nineteenth century, observed the importance of salt to the local people. Apart from adding to the taste of food, it was also viewed as a sign of wealth.

The Arab influence was not just restricted to trade. The spread of Islam was also important because it restricted the kind of meat that should be eaten. The eating of pork has always been seen as unclean by Muslims, but some groups of Muslims extend the same restrictions to other animals, such as amphibians. Many Africans, on the other hand, have traditionally eaten a wide variety of meat,

ranging from monkey to dog, crocodile to desert rat and zebra to elephant.

The level of European influence varies throughout the continent of Africa. For instance, relatively few Europeans settled in tropical Africa compared with East Africa because, it has been suggested, they feared the insects of the forest more than the larger wild animals of the plains.

The French, who colonized parts of West Africa, including Burkina Faso, the Ivory Coast and Togo left a strong tradition of French cooking, which can be seen in the large quantities of snails eaten. (There is, however, evidence that suggests that snails may have been eaten before French colonization.)

The Portuguese, who established the first permanent settlement of European origin south of the Sahara in Angola, in the sixteenth century, introduced cassava. They also introduced bananas, pineapples and peppers to East Africa. The British introduced strawberries and asparagus, as well as different breeds of cattle and sheep, to Kenya and Zimbabwe.

European cuisine can be found in restaurants and hotels in many parts of Africa. The baking of food is not common because very few Africans have ovens. On occasions Europeans have adapted local recipes to suit their own taste. For example, groundnut stew is sometimes eaten with sweet side dishes such as bananas and coconut, as well as chilli. However, the origins of eating sweet dishes with curries and stews can be traced back to Malaysian and Indian cuisine.

The British transported many Indians as indentured labour to East and southern Africa. Consequently, Indian cuisine is prominent in these regions and is reflected in such recipes as chicken *pilau*, curries, *shish kebab* and *roti* (Indian flat bread usually eaten with curries). Even before the British colonized parts of East Africa, the Indian, Arab and Portuguese traders had for centuries exchanged herbs and spices.

The growth in the numbers of prosperous urban Africans has led to an increase in western eating habits. Whereas rice and cassava may be eaten as many as three times a day by Africans from Sierra Leone to Tanzania, many Africans are eating different foods at breakfast, lunch and dinner in the same way as most Europeans and Americans.

Fast-food restaurants are beginning to develop in some African cities and they will certainly continue to influence what is eaten. The spread of television and the lifestyle it presents will also be an increasing influence.

A café in Mombasa, Kenya. The menu shows a variety of ethnic influences.

Regional specialities

West Africa

West Africa covers 3.84 million square km, or nearly five-sixths the size of the entire USA. The area is dissected by three major vegetational belts, each of which extends from east to west. The vegetation ranges from forest in the south, through grassland to desert in the north.

Climatic and religious differences can affect what is eaten. For example, in the semi-arid stretches of northern Nigeria or Mali millet or sorghum are likely to be consumed. Because these areas are also on the edge of the desert and, therefore, on the original Arab trade routes, much of the population is Muslim and, therefore, does not eat pork. In the lush interior areas of the Cameroons and Ghana, yam and

A little boy in Ife, Nigeria, selling okra.

Yam balls

You will need:

750 g yams
1 medium onion, finely chopped
1–2 medium tomatoes, peeled and finely
   chopped
2 eggs
25 g corned beef
¼ l groundnut oil
flour
salt
2 teaspoons of cayenne pepper

What to do:
(1) Peel the yams and boil until soft. Mash the cooked yams until smooth. Set aside. (2) The tomatoes can be peeled by placing them in boiling water. They should be removed with a slotted spoon, after which they are dipped in cold water. The skins are then very easy to remove. Fry half the tomatoes and onions in 80 ml of oil until soft. Place the mixture in a bowl with the yams, corned beef and the remaining tomatoes and onions, mix well and add salt and cayenne pepper. Beat in the eggs. (3) Pour a little flour on to a clean surface. Take a small amount of the mixture, enough to make a yam ball the size of a table tennis ball, and roll into shape, using the palm of your hand and the floured surface. Repeat until all the mixture has been used. Heat the remaining oil and carefully place four or five of the yam balls in the oil at a time. (4) Remove with a slotted spoon when they are golden brown and drain on kitchen paper. Serve hot. Serves 4.

Safety note: Ask an adult to place the yam balls in the hot oil. Be careful when chopping the tomatoes and onions, or ask an adult to chop them for you.

A factory in Freetown, Sierra Leone, where palm nut oil is produced and bottled.

plantain grow particularly well. They are often pounded to make *fufu*.

West Africa is the main area for the cultivation of groundnuts. From 1975 to 1977, West African exports of groundnuts contributed 17 per cent of the total world trade. Groundnut soup or stew is widely eaten in this region and the stew can also be found on the menus of some restaurants in Europe and the USA. Groundnuts are also processed to make cooking oil and peanut butter.

The use of fish and meat in the same dish is not uncommon in West Africa. *Paleva* sauce is one example of this custom. Dried or smoked fish like mackerel, sole or herring is mixed with lamb or beef and cooked in palm oil. The palm oil not only gives the dish a strong flavour but it also gives the dish a rich, deep-orange appearance. A green vegetable such as okra, cassava or bitter leaves, is also added to the stew. If *lubi* (rock potash) is added during cooking, the okra takes on a sticky, rather slimy consistency; it also prevents the palm oil from separating from the water. *Paleva* sauce is usually eaten by picking up the stew with a small ball of *fufu*.

Palm oil is native to West Africa. The palms are not usually cultivated; they are allowed to grow in a semi-wild state. One of the main advantages of palm oil is that is contains vitamins not present in other refined cooking oils. It does

A typical Ugandan meal of matoke *(plantain), sweet potatoes (yams) and meat stew.*

not have to be cooked and is used in the preparation of salads. Because of this, good quality palm oil is expensive.

Egusi (melon) seeds are used in the preparation of many dishes. Fish or meat dishes benefit from their addition. They add texture and colour, but their main purpose is to thicken the stew. *Egusi* seeds contain protein and oil. Many of the stews and soups are very hot. Red pepper is used in a lot of dishes and it can give a fiery quality.

East Africa

East Africa is very close to the equator but the temperature and rainfall vary considerably throughout the region. The mountains enable a greater variety of crops to be grown than in West Africa. Plants that require cooler temperatures can be planted high on the mountainsides, while coffee, tea and potatoes are grown in the foothills. East Africa produces 32 per cent of the world's tea and 7 per cent of its coffee.

In Mozambique a sauce known as *periperi* is eaten. The sauce is made from red peppers (capsicum), which are either used freshly chopped or ground. The sauce, or marinade, is made by mixing the juice of lemons, garlic, parsley and oil with the red peppers. The resulting sauce is hot and spicy and is used on both fish and meat. One of the favourite dishes made with *periperi* is called chicken Zambezia. When this dish is made coconut milk is used for the marinade instead of lemon juice. It is made by marinading (soaking) chicken pieces in *periperi* and then cooking the chicken over a charcoal fire. The chicken is usually served with freshly made *periperi* sauce.

The Ugandans prepare many dishes using plantain (*matoke*). Slices of plantain are cooked in large pots with fish or meat, onions and tomatoes. Spices and pepper are added for taste. The dish is served hot and is eaten on its own. The plantain gives the dish a slightly sweet flavour. The dish is called *matoke n'yama*, when made with meat, or *matoke ngege* if fish is used.

The wetter, coastal regions of East Africa, which have sandy soil, provide the region with the basic ingredient of many of its recipes: coconuts. The white part of the coconut is sometimes shredded and is a distinctive part of many dishes. Shredded coconut and vegetables are cooked with a variety of spices. Coconut milk can be obtained by grating the white part of the coconut, placing the gratings in a cloth and pouring hot water over them. The gratings are then squeezed two or three times in the cloth and the result is a milky liquid. Coconut milk is used in many recipes. Coconut is also used as a basis for desserts and sweets.

Even though 98 per cent of the

Coconut is used as a main ingredient and flavouring for many dishes in Africa.

population of East Africa is of African origin, Indian cuisine is also very popular. Curries and chapatis are eaten regularly in Kenya and Uganda. Prawn *pilau* is a combination of rice and prawns to which a variety of herbs and spices has been added during cooking, including garlic, cardamoms and cloves. Chicken is used as an alternative to prawns. (Tanzania, which includes the islands of Zanzibar and Pemba, produces 25 per cent of the world's cloves.)

Central Africa

As in West Africa, groundnuts appear in a variety of recipes. Spinach or greens prepared with peanut butter produce a stew that has a thick consistency and nutty flavour. This vegetarian dish from the Central African Republic is either eaten with rice or with pounded cornmeal (*bidia*).

Groundnuts give meat or fish dishes a strong flavour, thick consistency and a deep reddish-brown colour. A variety of dishes are made with groundnuts, including biscuits, salads and bread.

In Zimbabwe groundnuts are a major ingredient of *dovi*, which is peanut-butter stew that consists of chicken, greens, onions, pepper and tomatoes. It differs from its West African counterpart in that

The harvesting of ground nuts. They are more popularly known as peanuts.

greens and green peppers are included in the recipe. The Zimbaweans also like *sosaties*. This is marinated lamb that is cooked on a *braai* (barbecue). This is a popular party dish with people of European origin and with middle-class Africans.

Salt fish is a favourite of Angolans. The use of salt to preserve meat or fish has been used for centuries. It gives the fish a rather dry texture and a salty taste, even after the fish has been soaked for long periods. The flaked salt fish is cooked in a large pot or skillet

Groundnut cookies

You will need:

450 g roasted groundnuts
2 tablespoons of sugar

1 tablespoon of lemon juice
200 ml water

What to do:

(1) Pour the water into a pan and add sugar. Bring to the boil and then allow to simmer. (2) When the liquid becomes sticky, add the groundnuts and the lemon juice. Stir the mixture continuously. (3) When the mixture is very sticky, turn off the heat and pour the mixture into a greased cake tin. Spread the mixture out with a spatula. Set aside and allow to cool. (4) Then cut into pieces.

Drying fish in the sun is a popular and effective method of preserving fish.

with potatoes, green peppers and onions and it is served with boiled eggs and olives. Vegetable, meat or fish stews have strong flavours which make up for the rather bland taste of the *nsima*, *bidia* or *ugali*. Groundnuts, beans, greens, chilli pepper and spices are all used to add flavour and texture.

Food for special occasions

There is a wide range of festivals and special occasions that take place throughout Africa. There are many different kinds of ceremonies to celebrate religious or traditional occasions. In some places there are special initiation ceremonies to mark the change from childhood to adulthood. After an initiation ceremony, young Masai men drink the blood of a bullock before eating a meal of meat and milk. The Kikuyu people of Kenya barbecue *mahu* (the entrails of a sheep) or *mara* (the small intestine of a cow) stuffed with onions and the blood

Muslim boys lead home a sheep to feed the family for the feast of Eid following Ramadan.

of the slaughtered animal on special occasions. Because the dish is very rich, it is usually eaten on its own.

The eating of meat in many areas is a sign of a celebration because it is an expensive food. In parts of West Africa *jollof* rice is prepared for special occasions. The amount and quality of the meat in the dish is considered an indication of the wealth and status of the host. This dish can also be prepared from leftover food, but it is usual to start with fresh ingredients if the meal is in honour of special guests.

In some West African countries the followers of Islam make up over 80 per cent of the population. In 1981 more Muslims made the pilgrimage to Makkah from Nigeria than from any other country. Muslims observe Ramadan, the festival which occurs during the ninth month of the Muslim calendar, and fast between the hours of dawn and dusk. Before sunrise only a small meal is eaten, but after sunset they are allowed to take a full meal. In Africa a main meal will consist of meat or fish with rice or some other staple.

The feast of sacrifice takes place at the end of the pilgrimage to Makkah, and is marked by the slaughter of an animal. Africans who can afford it may slaughter a bullock rather than the traditional

Jollof Rice (*Benachin*)

You will need:

½ kg chicken, cut off the bone
225 g beef
4 medium onions, sliced
1 teaspoon of cayenne pepper
2 large tomatoes, peeled and sliced
3 dessert spoons of tomato purée
3 cloves of garlic, crushed
½ l groundnut oil
½ small cabbage, finely chopped
1 large aubergine, diced
250 g carrots, sliced
salt and black pepper to taste
450 g white rice
1–1¼ l water or stock

What to do:

(1) Wash and then cut the chicken and beef into small pieces. Season with salt, black pepper and crushed garlic. Allow to stand for half an hour. Wash and prepare the vegetables. (2) In a large, thick-based saucepan, fry the chicken in hot oil until golden. Set aside. Fry the beef in the same oil until quite brown. Add the onions and fry until brown. Add the tomatoes and tomato purée and simmer for 15 minutes. Carefully pour in the water (or stock) and bring to the boil. Add all the prepared vegetables, chicken and salt. Simmer for 30 minutes. (3) Remove the vegetables, beef and chicken with a slotted spoon and place them in a warm oven (50°C, 122°F, Gas Mark 1). Add rice to the pan and cook over a low heat until most of the liquid is absorbed and the rice is soft. (4) Put the rice on a plate with the chicken and the vegetables on top.
Serves 4–5.

Safety note: Care should be taken when frying the beef and chicken.

lamb sacrifice. Not all the followers can afford to slaughter an animal for this special occasion. It is normal for a portion of the slaughtered animal to be offered to the poor.

Christians celebrate the festivals of Easter and Christmas. It is not unusual for traditional Christmas dinners of turkey, roast potatoes, greens and Christmas pudding to be eaten. Africans who follow other traditions may still celebrate Christmas Day but eat alternative dishes. The Senegalese prepare a dish called *Yassa* for special occasions. It is made by marinating chicken in garlic, cloves and spices, after which the chicken is fried and then allowed to simmer in the marinade. It is presented on a large plate accompanied by rice and the guests sit in a circle and eat the meal

Masai men bleed a calf. At special ceremonies, young Masai men drink the blood.

with their hands.

Meals for special occasions may also include prepared desserts. Apart from fresh fruit with ice cream, dishes in which coconut is a main ingredient are popular in parts of East and West Africa. If someone has an oven, they are able to cook a wider variety of desserts, such as cassava cake, groundnut biscuits and coconut biscuits.

The popular West African dish, jollof *rice.*

Drinks

There are many natural drinks that are available to Africans which require very little preparation. In many parts of sub-Saharan Africa tropical fruits are readily available. Pineapples, oranges, paw paw and lemons make refreshing drinks.

A man and a woman making pombe, *which is beer made from fermented maize.*

Ginger beer

You will need:

450 g ginger
the juice of 2 lemons or limes
1 tablespoon of whole cloves
3½ l boiling water
3½ l cold water
4 tablespoons of sugar

What to do:

(1) Peel the ginger. Grind in a food processor (or grate it). (2) Place in a large glass heat-resistant container or large saucepan. Add sugar and cover with the boiling water. Allow to stand for one hour. (3) Strain the liquid through a cloth or a fine sieve. Mix in the lime or lemon juice and half of the cloves and add the cold water. Allow to stand for another hour. Strain the mixture at least once more. Stir in the remaining cloves. The mixture should be stored in a refrigerator. (4) It can be diluted to taste.

A Sierra Leonean boy carrying gourds full of palm wine. Palm wine is tapped from trunks of a particular species of palm tree.

Coconut milk is widely drunk. The Tanzanians do not bother to prepare coconut milk, but instead they knock a hole at either end of a green coconut and drink the contents.

In the semi-arid areas nomadic groups such as the Masai or the Fulani rely on goat, cow or camel milk. The Masai store the fresh or curdled milk in long, highly decorated gourds. They often mix the milk with cows' blood. Goat and camels' milk is richer and has a more delicious taste than cows' milk. Camels' milk is particularly good for babies because it has a low fat content and, therefore, is easily digested.

Local home-made alcoholic drinks are produced from a variety of sources. Many of them are produced from the fermentation of corn, millet or maize and they vary considerably in their alcoholic content. *Pito* is made in this way and is drunk in forested regions around Kumasi in central Ghana and in Nigeria.

Palm wine comes from the sap of a particular species of palm tree, which also provides palm nuts and palm oil. It is obtained by tapping the trunk of a palm. It is naturally alcoholic and has a white, slightly opaque and frothy appearance.

Although western-style alcoholic drinks are available, well-known brands can be difficult to obtain because some African countries cannot afford to import them. Many of the international brewers and soft drink manufacturers have set up factories in African countries in order to increase the sales of their products.

Alternatives to the usual range of spirits are also being explored by African countries. In Kenya tropical fruit such as paw paw is fermented and the Ghanaians produce a coconut liqueur.

Coffee is grown in the three

regions and is a popular hot drink. Tea is grown in East Africa and Angola. In parts of West Africa the leaves of different plants are used to make tea. For example, the people of Sierra Leone make tea from the leaves of a plant which they describe as the 'tea bush', which has large green leaves.

There are special rituals that are associated with the drinking of tea in some communities. The people of the southern Saharan area, who are mainly of Arab descent, perform a complicated ritual when they make tea. First they wash the tea in boiling water, which they then throw away. Next they add sugar and mint leaves before adding more boiling water. They leave the tea to stand and then they pour it into small glasses. They do not drink the tea – they return it to the pot and pour it again. This they do several times before they finally drink the tea. The exact process is started all over again, using the same tea but adding more sugar. This ritual is repeated until everyone has had three cups of tea: the first is the strongest, the next weaker and sweeter and the final cup weaker still. This ritual occurs two or three times a day and is very time consuming.

The pouring of tea is an important ritual in the southern Saharan area.

Lemon grass drink

You will need:

125 g lemon grass
(Fresh lemon grass can be bought from good supermarkets. It is also possible to buy dried lemon grass from specialist food shops.)
1 l water
sugar to taste

What to do:

Wash the lemon grass. Put it into a pan. Boil the water in a kettle. Pour it into the pan with the lemon grass and cover. Allow to stand for 6–8 minutes. Add sugar.

Safety note: Be very careful when pouring the hot water. Ask an adult to help.

Glossary

Amphibian An animal which lives both on land and in water.

Benachin A Gambian word for *Jollof* rice.

Bitter leaf A large shrub that grows in the tropics. It is related to chicory and lettuce.

Cassava A starchy root vegetable, grown throughout the tropics. It originates from South America.

Cuisine A style or type of cooking.

Cultivate To grow plants or vegetables.

Groundnuts More commonly known as peanuts. They can be eaten raw or roasted. When ground and added to stews, they act as a thickener.

Indentured labour A contract in which a person is bound to his or her master.

Islam The religion which follows the teachings of Muhammad.

Makkah A holy city: birthplace of Muhammad.

Matoke Ugandan word for plantain.

Phoenician A person from the ancient place of Phoenicia in Syria.

Pilau An Asian dish made with chicken and rice.

Plantain A tropical plant which produces a fruit similar to that of the banana tree.

Pulses Beans or peas.

Rite A religious ceremony.

Sisal A fibre made from the leaves of a tree.

Skillet A thick-based frying pan.

Sorghum A tropical cereal grass. It is sometimes known as Guinea corn and is widespread throughout Africa.

Tapioca Large white grains, which are obtained by heating cassava. Usually used to make puddings.

Yam The root of a tropical climbing plant. It belongs to the potato family.

Further Reading

Anthonio, H.O. and Isoun, M. *Nigerian Cookbook* (Macmillan, 1982)

Baeta, Barbara *West African Favourites* (Moxon Paperbacks, 1972)

Baley, Monica *Black Africa Cookbook* (Determined Productions, Inc, 1977)

Dede, Alice *Ghanian Favourite Recipes* (Anowuo Educational Publications)

Dovlo, F., Grimble, R. and Orraca-Tetteh R. *What Shall We Eat?* (Asempa Publishers, 1985)

Eldon, Kathy and Mullen, Eamon *Tastes of Kenya* (Kenway Publications, 1987)

Grant, Rosamund *Caribbean and African Cookery* (Grub Street, 1988)

Hultman, Tami (Ed.) *The African News Cookbook* (Penguin, 1985)

Olahore, Ola *African Cooking* (W. Foulsham & Co Ltd)

Ominde, Mary *African Cookery Book* (Heinemann, 1975)

General Reading

Jacobsen, P.O. and Kristensen, P.S. *A Family in West Africa* (Wayland, 1985)

Khalfan, Zulf M. and Amin, Mohamed *We Live in Kenya* (Wayland, 1983)

Mazrui, Ali *The Africans: A Triple Heritage* (BBC Publications, 1986)

Rodney, Walter *How Europe Underdeveloped Africa* (Bogle L'Ouverture, 1972)

Index

Picture acknowledgements

The publishers would like to thank the following for their permission to reproduce copyright pictures: J. Allen Cash Photolibrary 18, 25, 26, 28; Bruce Coleman 4, 8, 10, 14, 35, 40 (top); John & Penny Hubley 16, 23, 30, 33; Hutchison Library 11, 12, 13, 29, 37, 41, 44; Paul Misso 40 (bottom); Tropix 20; Christine Osborne *cover* 6, 7, 17, 21, 32, 34, 38, 43. The map on page 5 is by Thames Cartographic. The recipe illustrations are by Juliette Nicholson.